CCSS Genre Nonfiction

☑ **W9-BER-721**

? Essential Question
Who helps you?

Helping Me, Helping You!

by Cynthia Moloney

Chapter 1

Who Helps Me in My Family?

People help us every day. Some helpers are the people in our family. Some are not.

Who helps you? How do they help you?

There are many kinds of helpers.

(tl) Jeremy Woodhouse/Blend Images/Getty Images, (tc) Chev Wilkinson/Stone/Getty Images, (tr) CORBIS, (bl) Ocean/CORBIS, (br) Kai Chiang/Golden Pixels LLC/Corbis, (bkgd) Andrew Howe/Photodisc/Getty Images

My mother makes my breakfast in the morning. Then she walks to school with me.

Mom helps me read hard words.

I like spending time with Mom.

sidewalk

basketball

My brother walks me home from school.

My brother is my friend. We shoot baskets. He helps me dunk the ball. *Swoosh!*

In Other Words play basketball. En español: *jugamos baloncesto.*

My father cooks dinner. He <u>fixes</u> things, too. I help him.

Dad taught me how to ride my bike. I wear a helmet to be safe.

Language Detective

<u>Fixes</u> is an action verb. Find another action verb on this page.

helmet

My dad helps me learn new things.

My grandmother shows my picture to her friends. Grandma loves me. She will always accept me.

Grandma helps me knit a scarf.

scarf

Grandma makes me feel special.

STOP AND CHECK

Who helps fix things?
Who makes breakfast?

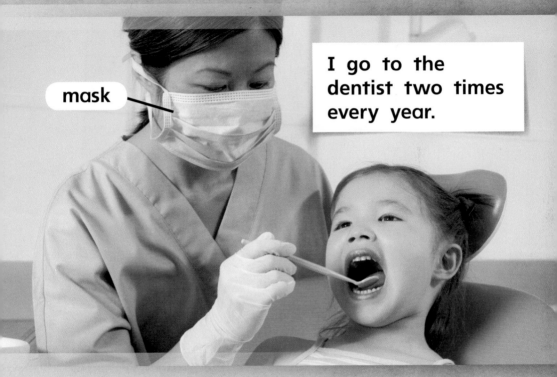

mask

I go to the dentist two times every year.

My dentist cleans my teeth. She shows me how to brush my teeth.

She says, "Don't eat candy too often!"

Language Detective	My is a possessive pronoun. Find another possessive pronoun on page 6.

librarian

Use a computer to find a book.

The librarian helps me choose books. She also shows me how to find books <u>on my own</u>. I love the library!

In Other Words by myself. En español: *por mi cuenta.*

My <u>sitter</u> meets me after school. She helps me with my homework.

We talk and play games. I have fun with my sitter!

In Other Words nanny. En español: *niñera.*

sitter

A sitter is a person who takes care of you.

Firefighters put out fires. Firefighters teach me what to do if there is a fire. They say, "Go outside and call 9-1-1."

fire truck

A firefighter teaches kids to be safe.

hard hat

Builders wear hard hats to stay safe.

Builders help me. They build stores and offices. They build big hospitals and small playgrounds.

Who helps you?

STOP AND CHECK

How does a dentist help?
How does a sitter help?

CORBIS

Respond to Reading

Retell

Use your own words to retell *Helping Me, Helping You!*

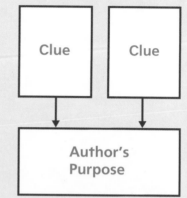

Text Evidence

1. Look at Chapter 2. Who helps you? Author's Purpose

2. Why do you think the author wrote this book? Author's Purpose

3. How do you know that *Helping Me, Helping You!* is nonfiction? Genre

Compare Texts
Read more about firefighters.

FIRE!

Brett Panelli/Stone/Getty Images

13

Loud bells clanging
In our ears,
We hurry up
And grab our gear.
Engines screaming
In the night.
Ladders stretching
Out of sight.

Orange flames light
Up the air.
Clouds of smoke blow
Everywhere.
Gushing water
Sprays about.
Now we've put the
Fire out!

Make Connections

Look at both selections. How can
helpers help you? Text to Text

Focus on

Social Studies

Purpose To find out about people who help you

What to Do

 Step 1 ▶ Work with a partner. Talk about people who help you.

Step 2 ▶ Draw a chart. List the people who help you.

Who Helps Me	How They Help
Mom	Cooks food

Step 3 ▶ Draw a picture showing how someone you know helps you. Write a sentence about the person. Share with the class.